WILBUR

The Great Horned Owlet's

RESCUE

WILBUR
The Great Horned Owlet's
RESCUE

JEANETTE MAYO-UPHOLZ

outskirts
press

In Memory Of
David, Jennifer, and
Carolyn

Dedication

To the Wonder of Creation

and

All

There

Is

Within

The more I study nature, the
more I am amazed at the
Creator — Louis Pasteur

Table of Contents

Introduction

Countless forms of beauty and life can be found in all that exists in the vastness of nature, which is defined as the collective physical world. Included are animals, plants, landscapes, products, and activity of the earth, the sea, and the universe. Humankind has dominated over much of it and protecting and preserving it to the best of our ability should be a priority. How else can it still be here for future generations?

Although humanity is part of nature, it is often considered a separate category. We share our world with the animal kingdom, and both of us depend on it for life, making us interconnected as inhabitants of the earth. They have a wondrous ability to survive independently of humans but the fact remains that any of them can have problems, both as a whole and as individuals. These can stem from the natural consequences of aging, disease, and injury.

Also, it is recognized that, over the millennia, there have been plentiful and very painful factors that have contributed to their demise. These include such things as their natural habitat giving way to towering cities and sprawling development, wildlife exploitation, pollution, invasive species, and chemical contamination. The list goes on. As a result, many species have become extinct while others continue to dwindle. It is our duty to understand how they are affected by these negative influences and what we can do to address their needs and alleviate the problems.

Fortunately, in many of the venues, human intervention has been beneficial in recognizing and remedying some of these consequences. Nevertheless, an overabundance of challenges are ever-present and so the crusade continues.

There is a fortuitous survival outcome to tell regarding the mishap of a lone great horned owlet. On one micro fraction of our total planet, at just the right time, I discovered a newly born owlet on the ground, still alive. It was an ordinary day for me, up to that point; then, surprise extraordinaire! And so, this story unfolds.

That single moment quickly impelled me to reach out to the local nature center to get him the emergency care and rehabilitation that he needed. After they provided him with a night of much TLC, the tiny owlet recovered. They also contacted other resources that could possibly help in their plan to return him to his very high nest. When they collaborated their skills, their endeavors were strengthened and they became successful. Thanks to everyone's dedication and determination to save the helpless creature, of the estimated 3.9 million great horned owls in the United States and Canada, this one, in particular, was given a second chance to grow and mature.

Highlighted days like these on the calendar of life show how any given day can greet us with an unexpected venture. Then, too, there is that reward at the end of the day when it involves reaching out and contributing to making other lives better (human or creatures). Something like this can come along anytime, anywhere, any way, and you could be at the receiving or giving end. Either way, it has the effect of changing our perspective and helping to make our worries of everyday living seem less overpowering.

Even though we are busy doing the things "we have to do," which may be all consuming and distracting, taking the time to enjoy the things "we'd like to do" helps keep our lives balanced. Looking to nature can promote that equilibrium when we become more synchronized with the natural world we live in.

So, regardless of whether you are a nature lover or someone of a varying degree on the scale, we are here on our plentiful planet together. When we view the stars above, they are the same stars that twinkle for everyone and for every living thing far beyond us. Undeniably, we are never alone; rather, we are there for each other. Would you agree?

Since we never know what is in store for us, it is with hope that today may bring a new and positive experience into our lives.

Whatever that may be, when it comes as a surprise, it offers us an opportunity to do something good, in kind, to contribute to life. While striving to do so, persistence helps to achieve our goal(s), realizing that the good outweighs the struggles. Whatever your ambitions are, consider them as achievable and seek them with enthusiasm even though they may seem elusive.

These various thoughts have common threads of optimism and inspiration. We can often seek and find these qualities in one another, in our everyday lives, and in nature. They can be found in Wilbur's story. You can empathize with his rescuers concerning the difficulty of their situation and, in the desire to help, imagine yourself as part of the group effort.

Acknowledgments

There are those people who helped and supported me in the development of this book and those who were involved in the rescue that generated the story. I wish to express my deep gratitude for each of their distinct contributions because without them, this book would not have been composed.

My husband, John, was always supportive and constructive with proofreading, no matter how many times I asked for his assistance. His insight and feedback were of tremendous help, and he gave me the incentive to keep going with the book. I thank him for his loving support, steadfast patience when I spent many early mornings or late nights at the computer, doing extra chores and for doing it all so wholeheartedly.

My son, Brian, championed me to pursue creating the book when I first expressed thoughts about it, shortly after the rescue. Whenever there were glitches with the computer, questions about documents, or

giving technical guidance, he was promptly available to answer questions and help work through problems. His loving support, reassurance, and wisdom always bring me joy and comfort, more than he realizes.

Marianne and Lois, beloved friends for decades, were interested in and enthusiastic about the book from its very early stages to the finish. Their perspective as readers of the preliminary manuscript, and words of encouragement helped me to move forward while completing it. Always being there to listen and giving their heartfelt opinions and thoughts meant a great deal to me.

The Denison Pequotsepos Nature Center,
Mystic, Connecticut
Executive Director of Operations:
Davnet Conway
Animal Curator: Lori Edwards

Davnet and Lori were always gracious and willing to take time out from their busy schedules to be of assistance with paperwork and offer resourceful information. Also, as readers of the early manuscript, their input and enthusiasm were of great import and pivotal.

They also provided many photographs of Wilbur and the ongoing rescue, so wonderful for all to see.

Quiambaug Volunteer Fire Company,
    Stonington, Connecticut
Captain/Vice President/T-29:
    Theresa A. Hersh

Theresa demonstrated resolve and diligence about pursuing a means to access the nest. After determining the fire company's truck was too large to navigate parts of the road leading to it, she speedily initiated assistance from a tree company that had been working nearby in the neighborhood. Her timely actions were certainly a prime factor in the success of the rescue.

The Tennett Tree Service,
    Windham, Connecticut
Bucket-lift Operator: Cory Higgins
Ground Man: Jeffrey Stachura
Office Manager: Jen Stone

When Cory and Jeffrey were informed about the owlet's dilemma, they eagerly responded and came immediately to

evaluate their ability to access the nest. They concluded they could and within minutes, proceeded with the plan. Their profession-alism and extreme efforts were paramount in safely and successfully returning the owlet home. As soon as Cory placed him in the nest, he took a photo of him and the second owlet that was there - a rare sight to see – look for it in the book.

Jen cordially gave her assistance in processing the paperwork for consent forms which I greatly appreciated.

Stonington Volunteer Ambulance
    Corps, Inc., Stonington, CT
Commander/EMT: Julia M. Stoner
Julia's presence was reassuring for everyone's morale knowing there would be ready assistance, if needed, during the extremely high bucket-lift maneuvers.

For all other people behind the scenes who helped make the completion of the rescue a reality, your input was necessary and appreciated.

Outskirts Press, Inc.

Publishing Consultant: Allison

Author Representative: Lisa

Editor: Barbara

Designer: Michelle

They guided me every step of the way with clear and precise direction in the development of this book, enabling the entire process to advance smoothly and be enjoyable.

Wilbur's Rescue

When we are fortunate enough to have shared good times with others while working toward a common goal, it can become one of our most meaningful and satisfying memories. On an otherwise average day, that is just what came about, when the following true-life event developed into an awesome experience for everyone involved. It all began with a baby bird that had fallen out of his nest, and the sequence of events that evolved from the moment I found him until his ultimate return home.

Many caring people joined together and gave a tremendous amount of effort to come to the aid of this tiny creature. They created a well-thought-out plan of action and remarkably were able to carry it out in less than twenty-four hours. During that time, they also had to ensure his safety and well-being.

This story follows the challenges they met and overcame, from the beginning to the finish of the rescue. It also introduces a whimsical portrayal of what the owlet was feeling and thinking throughout this time. Perhaps it will awaken the child that is within us all. He will begin:

Help, help, I've fallen out of my nest! I'm dropping so fast toward the ground, and it's such a great distance. Where will I land? Ouch, that was a sudden stop! It took the wind right out of me, making me feel a little bit dazed. It's best to lie still, catch my breath, and wait to see what happens next.

Where am I? Am I okay? Um, I guess so; I can move everything. I'm sure glad I landed on some grass and pine needles instead of rock; that would have been a lot worse.

To me, a lush carpet of pine needles or spongy grass is more luxurious than a Persian rug. — Helen Keller

It was a late afternoon in March 2019. The sky was mostly overcast, and a constant breeze was stirring, making it feel blustery and chilly. While walking outside to get the mail, I noticed a small mound of white fluff on the ground, and I couldn't imagine what it was. As I approached closer to it, I saw that it was a baby bird, although I had no idea what species. It was like a chick but different in some ways. It certainly seemed unusual to be born so early in the year.

He was lying on a grassy spot beneath a very tall white pine, probably the tree where his nest was. Because many branches were crisscrossing one another, the nest could not be spotted easily. With numerous trees in the yard, I was glad that he had been under one where I happened to be walking. And I was so lucky to find him then because if I had driven the car down to the mailbox, as is often the case, I would never have seen him.

My parents are panicking. I hear them frantically calling out as they see me helplessly lying here, not knowing how

Wilbur's Tree where his nest was located.

badly I might be hurt. And, sadly, it's not within Mom's natural ability to pick me up and move me. And I can't get back into the nest by myself now, but I could if I were just a little older and more vigorous. That's because we instinctively know how to use our claws and beak and flap our wings to help us climb back up a tree. It's quite a feat if I do say so myself, and is something to marvel at! It's not easy to believe unless you can see it.

I'm scared of being alone. What if I'm never found? Is anyone around? It seems I've been here for hours. Other birds are calling each other; I've heard their songs before, and they've been friendly.

Wait, what's that other noise? It sounds like the rustling of footsteps nearby. Will they wander this way or even notice me? I must try to get their attention. I'll call out (peep, peep, peep) — help, help, please; here I am, over here!

He seemed very still at first, but as I drew nearer, his legs moved slightly and he began to chirp softly, indicating that he was not seriously injured. So, hopefully, he would have an excellent chance to fully recover. His downy, cloudlike feathers rippled in the chilly breeze, exposing pinkish skin underneath. He was so beautiful. Seeing him in disbelief, my heart skipped a beat.

I could only think of how cold and alone he must have felt and wondered how long he had been there. It probably wasn't a great deal of time because nearby predators would most likely have found him fairly quickly.

It was captivating to gaze upon this stunning creature and remarkable that he had survived, considering the long distance he had fallen. He was so endearing that my first reaction was to pick him up, but then I decided not to, thinking perhaps his mother would reject him if she detected he had been held.

In all things of nature, there is something of the marvelous. —Aristotle

Anxious to get him the help he needed, I quickly went to tell my husband and then called the nearby Denison Pequotsepos Nature Center (DPNC). The center is well known and loved by the local community and beyond, and it provides tremendous service to wildlife when they are displaced, sick, and injured. To have the DPNC just a few miles away, with its staff's expertise, was a crucial factor in the survival of this tiny bird.

Oh no, why is she leaving already? Where is she going? Please, come back! I desperately need help! I should have moved more and chirped louder, but it's difficult to gather that much energy because I'm so tired, cold, and hungry.

After explaining to those at the nature center what happened, they became very excited and told us to bring him in right away so they could check him out. Although we were still concerned about handling him, it was necessary under the circumstances, so my husband went to get him while I finished talking on the phone and then looked for a container to put the baby bird in.

Oh, relief - I hear footsteps again, and they're coming straight toward me! Glad they only took a few minutes to return. It's somebody else, maybe her spouse? I don't know what he will do, but I know I must trust him. Oh, now he's picking me up and carrying me toward the house as he keeps telling me I'm going to be all right.

So far, so good. My parents are still calling although I can't see them.

As soon as my husband was back, we placed the little bird in a small box, telling him, as if he could understand us, not to worry because he would be getting help within minutes. We headed off, delighted to have the center's support, and know our little friend would receive the best care that he possibly could. We were optimistic that he would do well. But we would have to wait to learn from the nature center what they determined his true physical condition to be.

Without hesitation, we got into their car and left. I've never ridden like this before; what a strange way of getting about. Flying is much better! All during the drive, they gave me encouragement that I'd be okay.

Guess Mom and Dad are still watching and feel happy that I was found. But now

Denison Pequotsepos Nature
Center Welcome Sign. (DPNC)

they must feel troubled seeing me being taken away and thinking I may never come back.

Fortunately, we arrived at the nature center shortly before their five o'clock closing. If we had found him just fifteen minutes later, they would not have been open. Then, being that late in the day, who knows how much time it would have taken to track down other people who were able and willing to help. He needed immediate attention, and any delay would undoubtedly have been detrimental.

Well, that was a short drive. We arrived lickety-split at our destination, but I don't know where we are. What is this place? I see an inviting building in the middle of some beautiful woods. Indeed, there must be some other owls living in this area, maybe even some of my relatives. I will listen for some hooting.

Now, we've left the car and are on our way inside.

When we entered the premises, a staff member, who would be his caretaker, was waiting to receive the tiny bird. Much to our surprise, she identified him as a baby (owlet) great horned owl, and we were delighted to finally know what he was. She estimated he was just a day or so old and stated they are usually born in March. We handed him over to her, and she immediately went to examine him and put him into an incubator to warm him up. Because the center was closing, she would bring him home in order to feed him throughout the night.

Wilbur being fed.

Davnet Conway, Executive Director of Operations, DPNC hand feeding Wilbur. Davnet took care of Wilbur throughout the night on the day he was found, until his re-nesting the next day.

In the morning, the staff would re-evaluate his condition and determine the most appropriate course to take. Their number one preference would be to renest him as soon as possible, if he were well enough to do so. We kept our fingers doubly crossed and had high hopes for that to be the scenario.

It's hard to believe that I was found and taken to a creature-caring place where they are feeding me some delicious food and keeping me comfortable. Things are working out well, but I miss my family so much.

I've been thinking a lot about how Mom keeps me warm, especially in bad weather, and how Dad is such an expert hunter for our meals (sometimes Mom too). And they are constantly on guard to chase away predators. If only I could let them know I am being well cared for and I'm safe and sound, that would help put them at ease.

We then left, feeling relieved that the owlet would be getting all the attention that

DPNC Entrance.

he needed. Observing firsthand the nature center's readiness and action to care for him was heartening. It made me wonder how many creatures are in similar situations every day all over creation and sadly never get help when they need it.

Little did I know when I had awoken this morning that this enchanting owlet would come into our lives. And now it was time to give it a name. Even though I didn't know the bird's gender, I called him Wilbur, after the road where he lived. Welcome, wee Wilbur!

Shortly after arriving home, another DPNC staff member came to see the spot where Wilbur had been lying and the tree where the nest could be. It was important to gather as much information as possible to plan the best strategy for renesting him. Although the nest was well hidden, she was able to focus on it with the aid of her binoculars. She informed us the staff would call in the morning with an update on Wilbur and the plans, and then departed.

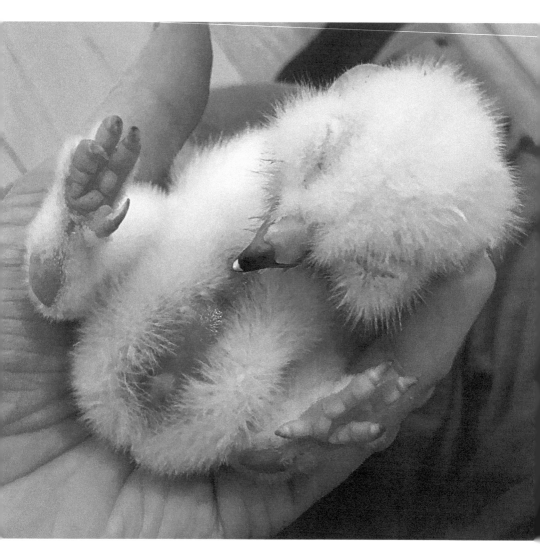

Wilbur.

Wilbur.

Later that evening, wanting to learn more about the great horned owl, I delved into the online information and discovered some fascinating facts about the species that I'd like to share with you as the story progresses.

Initially, we were happy to read that the parents accept their babies after being handled by humans since owls have little or no sense of smell. It was something we were concerned about after we had picked him up. In retrospect, had I known that when I found him, I would have picked him up immediately and put him inside my jacket. I do wish I had done that.

Additionally, they are one of the earliest nesters, beginning in January or February, and often take over a premade nest from crows, hawks, or squirrels, for example. They use a few of their feathers to line it. There are usually two or three eggs, often covered with snow since they are laid so early in the year (we wondered if there could be one or two other owlets alone in the nest). The mother tends to the nest

Adult Great Horned Owl in pine tree.

around the clock for about a month. Can you envision her sitting on the nest during long, heavy downpours or prolonged sleet or snowstorms? She surely is the epitome of patience and devotion. A few hours before hatching and emerging from their eggs, the owlets can be heard vocalizing (as other species also do). After the eggs hatch, both parents care for and feed the babies for up to several months. They have huge appetites and grow very fast for thirty-five to forty-five days. They mature at two years old and become one of the largest owls in the East. Females are larger than the males, weighing about four pounds and reaching about two feet tall. The males are about a pound less.

Early the following day, a DPNC staff member called to let us know that Wilbur's condition had greatly improved, much to everyone's delight. Based on his positive progress and, without further ado, the staff planned to proceed at once with their plan to renest him. Again, I must say, their enthusiasm to care for this stunning owlet was uplifting to see.

While in my bed, trying to fall asleep, it was difficult not to constantly think about plunging through the air like a rocket and crash-landing on the ground with a sudden impact. I couldn't recall why I had fallen out of the nest and questioned whether I could have done something differently to avoid it.

Eventually, since I was so exhausted from the day's trauma, I managed to fall asleep.

Then, as the early dawn was breaking, I awakened, and it was glorious to greet the morning. At first, it took me a moment to remember where I was, but then I recollected that my caretaker had taken me to her house last evening. After receiving all her help, I'm feeling so much better today. I'm sure glad she's still with me.

And now, I even have my own handmade "nest pouch" and a soft blanket that makes me feel comforted and wrapped up with love. And it was such a fun surprise to see the wonderful great horned owl stuffed toy lying beside me. It keeps me company, helps me feel at home, and is so huggable.

After a delicious breakfast, I noticed there was a lot to look at in my new surroundings, which were very welcoming and cheerful. Even so, I wondered how long I would be there and was bewildered by it all. As I pondered what else the day might bring, I still was groggy, so it seemed like a good time to take a siesta.

Shortly after they had called, staff members started arriving at our house to

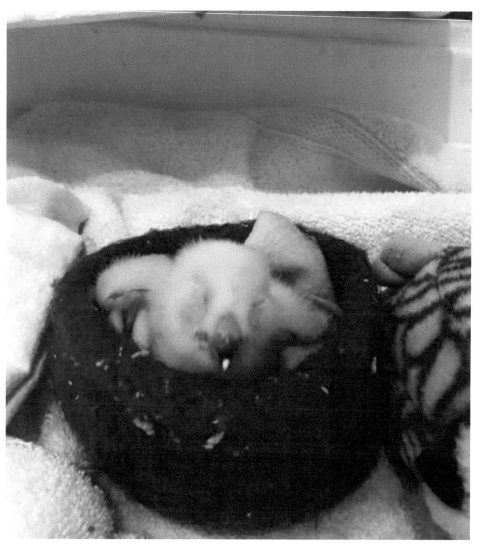

Wilbur with his Great Horned Owl stuffed toy beside him.

Wilbur with blanket and nest pouch.

determine the best way to proceed with their plan. They had asked the local fire department if they could come and gauge whether their fire engine with the tallest ladder might be able to reach the nest. The fire captain arrived, but unfortunately, it was concluded that because the road had a narrow, curved section, their ladder truck would not be able to navigate it.

With this disappointing news, the DPNC staff and other volunteers continued going forward to initiate another solution. They were on their cell phones checking out various resources, such as professional tree climbers and people with bucket-lift trucks. Their team spirit filled the air with a sense of intensity and resolve, knowing that time was of the essence for Wilbur's welfare. The sooner he was home, the better off he would be.

I wonder if everyone knows that the best thing for me is to get back to my family. And, since the nest is so very high, how will they get there? After all, I've never seen human beings going up into trees.

While the phone calls continued, a tremendous stroke of good luck came about when a tree service company with a bucket-lift truck was heard working farther down at the end of the road. It was perfect timing and an ideal opportunity to inquire if it was possible for them to assist us. The fire captain went to them and explained the situation, and after hearing about the problem, the workers gladly agreed to check out the site.

They came right away to ascertain the height of the nest and the maneuvers that would be necessary to reach it. Knowing the maximum range of their bucket lift was seventy-five feet and estimating the nest to be approximately seventy from the ground, was an important factor. Even though the operator would have to trim limbs on the way up, they thought that task would be manageable. And they were relieved that there was level terrain and ample space to position the truck at the base of the tree safely. Having assessed these conditions, they felt confident they could carry out the delicate quest. That was fantastic for everyone to hear, and we were so appreciative of their generosity in donating their time, labor, skills, and equipment.

The plan would now proceed without delay, and the phone calls seeking other resources could cease. The workers went to retrieve their truck. When they returned, they parked it as close to the tree as possible to prepare for a trial run (without Wilbur).

Once in place, the lift gradually ascended. As everyone was intensely watching it, there were moments when it seemed the nest would be too difficult to access taking into account the numerous branches blocking passage to it and its extreme height. But it soon became apparent, that owing to the highly skilled operator, progress was made little by little. He paused along the way to painstakingly use his chain saw and power trimmers to clear a path to the nest. When he safely arrived there, the lift was within just a couple feet of its maximum reach — an enormous stretch and a close call! Everyone sighed with relief seeing there was now a means to return Wilbur home.

Jeffrey Stachura, Ground Man: Tennett Tree Service.

Cory Higgins in bucket lift approaching nest.

To make this accomplishment even more exciting, when the operator looked inside the nest, wonderfully there was another owlet there. It was such a magical moment when he shouted the good news down to us that Wilbur had a sibling waiting there who appeared well (they must have been missing each other a lot). After hearing that, there was a concern for his physical condition also. Additionally, an eastern cottontail was there, which the parents had delivered earlier.

Meanwhile, Wilbur had been brought to the site earlier by his caretaker, and they were both patiently waiting to see what might happen next.

Goodness, look at all this hustle and bustle. There is a big, noisy truck with a bucket lift here that is in our tree. My family and I could never have imagined seeing something like this.

All the activity and noise of the trial run would be very alarming to Wilbur's parents. Regrettably, it was an unavoidable consequence that would cause them to either depart or defensively go after the

Davnet Conway, DPNC and Wilbur waiting in car.

Close up of Wilbur.

Bucket lift reaching Wilbur's nest.

Davnet Conway, DPNC and Theresa Hersh, Fire Captain, Quiambaug Volunteer Fire Department with Wilbur.

Left to Right: Julia Stoner, Theresa Hersh, Cassandra Meyer-Ogren, Davnet Conway, Cory Higgins, Jeffrey Stachura, Lori Edwards.

lift operator. Indeed, as he proceeded, they did leave, but thankfully, they soon were seen flying about and perching in nearby trees.

It's upsetting that all this commotion has frightened Mom and Dad so much that they left. My brother must be so scared and confused, too, besides feeling all alone. Oh my, our entire family is in such turmoil. I sure wish I could help make things better.

It was time to lower the lift and take that final big step of retrieving Wilbur.

Wait a minute, what's going on now? The bucket is coming back down. Is it for me? Oh yes, it seems so because everyone is saying, "Hooray, now we can get Wilbur." Wahoo! There, it's settled on the ground, and I can hardly wait to get in it.

The bucket lift was on the ground and all set to receive the fetching passenger, but before that occurred, the group wanted to take pictures of him with his fans. It was so engaging to see him with his blanket,

Left to right: Julia Stoner, Commander, Stonington Volunteer Ambulance; Theresa Hersh, Fire Captain; Davnet Conway, DPNC; Cory Higgins and Jeffrey Stachura, Tennett Tree Service.

looking so precious and quite photogenic. He seemed more attentive today, compared to his sleepiness yesterday. When he intermittently opened his eyes, taking in the view, it was as if he had somehow connected with his rescuers and was aware of their devotion to helping him.

I'm just seconds away from taking that big ride but before that happens, my friends would like to take some photos. That's fine, I'm sure it won't take too long. After all, they've done tons and tons for me, and I'd like to return a favor even though it's so small in comparison.

We're all getting into position now, and here I am, posing right in the middle of everyone. I'm being held by my caretaker and feel quite comfortable with my blanket. When first meeting her yesterday and every minute after, she has been such a super foster mom. I'm still wondering how she knows what my favorite foods are. It will be difficult for me to leave her.

Not knowing how long it would take either parent to return, the nature center staff

Top Row, Left to right: Cory Higgins and Jeffrey Stachura, Tennett Tree Service; Bottom Row, Left to right: Julia Stoner, Stonington Volunteer Ambulance Corps.; Theresa Hersh, Quiambaug Volunteer Fire Department; Jeanette Mayo-Upholz, Author; John R. Upholz, Husband; Davnet Conway and Lori Edwards, DPNC.

wanted to prepare a "warming sock," which consists of dry rice heated in a microwave oven and then put into a sock. We promptly assembled one, ready to give to the bucket operator the moment he left with Wilbur in hand. He would place it in the nest upon arrival to help keep both owlets warm while their parents were away.

When the brief photo session ended, Wilbur was at last handed over to the lift operator, along with the warming sock. Joy filled the air as we witnessed it, but it was a bittersweet moment as well, because we had to say goodbye to our fine, little fuzzy-feathered friend. There were eleven people present and it was great seeing how they had reached out with compassion for this little owlet. When they united and joined forces to usher Wilbur back to his abode, they attained an amazing feat. Fulfilling their goal was truly a triumph for all.

Well, the photos were fun, and it only took a few minutes. In two shakes of a lamb's tail, the operator was ready to take me to my nest. Thank you, thank you, buckets, and buckets! Even with all

Left to Right:

Denison Pequotsepos Nature Center
Staff Members: Cassandra Meyer-Ogren,
Laura Craver-Rogers, Lori Edwards.

the excitement of going home, it's not easy leaving my friends.

Here I go! I can't believe it's real! I realize now that everyone knew how much I needed to be back with my family and were so smart to figure how to get that done. And I'm not even afraid to take this ride because I trust them; after all, they saved my life! And, of course, I've never, ever been fearful of heights.

Wow, being inside the bucket sounds like a lot more racket than before when it was farther away. I won't let that upset me though because, look at what it's doing for my family and me. I'm eager to see my brother but also concerned that when the lift approaches a second time, he'll become even more frightened. Hopefully, once I'm there, we'll both feel better.

Up and away they rose, slowly but surely. All eyes from the ground were glued on them every inch of the way. As we watched with great anticipation, we were touched to see Wilbur getting lifted home while our spirits were lifted as well.

As we're going up, it seems like traveling through outer space, and yet the higher we go, the more familiar it appears as we get closer and closer to our destination. We're almost to the top of the tree, and I can see our nest now. I can't believe how lofty it is; it's a wonder I wasn't badly hurt after falling that far.

Owlet bodies are very soft and bouncy, which helps prevent severe injuries if they fall out of their nest. Owls do not push their young out as some birds do, so that would not be a danger for them. But they can be knocked out accidentally, or they can fall through an opening in it. One common reason is when enemies such as crows provoke the owls there often will be rigorous scuffles as the parents try to protect their young, who then get dislodged. Considering the abundance of crows living in the vicinity, there's a good chance that this kind of scrimmage accounted for Wilbur's plight.

Finally, the bucket lift arrived at the nest, and Wilbur was placed in it along with the

Nest showing Wilbur with sibling,
Warming Sock and rabbit.

warming sock; the moment we were waiting for. The operator had executed the arduous undertaking with flawless precision. The entire process couldn't have gone any smoother, even if it had been planned days in advance. With his job completed, he once again backed the bucket lift away and descended to the ground. Wilbur was such a courageous champion for the entirety of his harrowing misfortune. That likely helped his parents feel somewhat relieved to see he was not filled with fear, as they kept their eyes on him from yonder.

At last, I'm home! My wish came true, and I feel so over the moon about it! I hope Mom and Dad can see how happy I am now! It's incredible to be back with my brother and see he's in good shape. We greeted each other with open wings and gladness of heart. He said, "Wilbur, Wilbur, are you okay?" I replied, "I'm fit as a fiddle." We were so invigorated that we wanted to do a jig, but there was so much to talk about, so we started to chitter and chatter. What a tale of caution I had to tell him about the danger of falling out of the nest!

As the lift disappeared from our sight, I thought to myself, "How many teeny birds like me have ever ridden in a huge bucket lift to a height of over seventy feet?" How many in the whole wide world? That will be a good conversation piece for our family to hoot about for years to come. And how could I forget the comforting warming sock being there too?

We fretted over where Mom and Dad could be because there still were no signs of them. Were they too terrified to ever return? That thought made us quiver with fear, imagining what could happen to us without their protection.

On a more positive note, I wanted to believe they had been able to watch what was going on from a distance and they understood that I was being helped. I know our parents love us very much and have a lot of patience, so they would wait until things quieted down before returning. We are praying for that. The uncertainty though is overwhelming. For now, we don't know what else to do except try to stay calm and trust that our parents will be back.

Within minutes, everyone prepared to leave the scene as quietly and quickly as possible to encourage Wilbur's parents to return. One by one, Wilbur's friends quietly departed. In what seemed to be no time at all, total tranquility prevailed, the opposite of when commotion permeated most of the morning. Each person took with them winning memories of Wilbur's story and the vital contribution they gave in the daunting task of the rescue. Collectively, they were a superhero, having a life-saving impact on him.

You could sense the emotions in the air; that of unity and comradery for a job well done. There was also a hint of sadness for having to leave Wilbur forever.

We noticed all the people and vehicles start to leave. The only noise now is the cawing of nearby crows. We're on edge about them and shudder to think they may come to badger us just as they've done in the past.

Owls are the crows' most dangerous predator, and an agitated group of crows often will torment them. That was exhibited at the site unintentionally when a recording of a great horned owl's hooting was played on a cell phone. Within a minute, about a dozen crows appeared out of the blue and noisily circled above the tree where the nest was. It certainly was not anticipated that they would be able to hear and react to the recording. It was nerve-racking to see, but to our great relief, they departed after several minutes.

My brother and I continued chattering on and nestled together against the warming sock. We were a lot more relaxed and ready for a snooze after such a whirlwind day. Silently lingering in my mind were the thoughts that I must not panic; I must be courageous, be strong, and have faith that I can do this.

After everyone was gone, it was as if nothing had taken place. My husband and I went back to the house and waited on the front porch to keep a diligent lookout for the parents' return. Then, incredibly, in less than an hour, we spotted them flying into their tree. It was an exhilarating sight to witness, knowing it was of great significance for the survival and well-being of the two owlets. We couldn't ask for anything more and were so excited to report the good news to the nature center staff, so we immediately phoned them.

We were not asleep for long before I started to awaken, feeling that I was still dreaming about hearing Mom and Dad's familiar greetings. But when I fully awoke, I couldn't believe my eyes: they were right there before me! It wasn't a dream after all; my prayers and faith that they'd come back to us came true.

Dad was sitting on a nearby branch, seeming well pleased. Mom came into the nest and tenderly wrapped her wings around us, and we enthusiastically chirped with glee. What a glorious homecoming; it was like we were on top of the world! Then I told them about everything that had happened since yesterday. They said they could watch a lot of it but when we were leaving in the car, they became puzzled not knowing where we were going.

It was good to hear that they were able to tend to my brother throughout the night. The next morning, when all the busyness began, and the bucket lift appeared, they left the nest but remained close enough to see what was happening.

Mom and Dad told me they were exceedingly proud of me throughout it all. I explained that at first I was afraid but I soon overcame my fear because I realized how kind and loving my rescuers were. They responded, "Wilbur, besides being such a brave son, you're a very wise little owlet as well." It was comforting for me to hear that.

Soon, we were all quite hungry, and it was time to eat. There was rabbit for dinner, and it was great to have a fresh-caught meal. We eat nothing but meat and usually have a good variety, such as rodents, small mammals, birds, and waterfowl. Skunk is even on our menu; because of our poor sense of smell, we are not bothered by its odor.

My mind wandered a little as I pictured when my brother and I would be old enough to hunt like our parents. It would be fun to have a contest with him to see who could catch something first.

The hours slipped away as we talked about what we each had gone through, and the four of us rejoiced at the exceptional deeds my rescuers did to bring me home. Being so weary from it all and glad that it was behind us, we settled in for the night and were utterly content and at peace. Before we realized it, the shadows lengthened as dusk steadily approached and the busy world became serene.

As darkness descended, Dad prepared for the long night and planned on getting more food for later (my brother and I are always looking for snacks) while Mom tenderly kept us warm. Nighttime is our favorite time to hunt because our vision is better then, but we will also go at other times of the day. Our acute sense of hearing is an additional aid in helping us to be very effective in locating and tracking prey.

The moonlight shimmered brightly, and its glow reflected in our eyes. As the wind played around and about, the pine trees responded in unison with a rustling, soothing sound, one we often hear and love. Life couldn't be better, and we had so much hope for the future. We were looking forward to a bright new day; tomorrow was on its way.

As we looked to the heavenly sky and viewed the twinkling stars, we whispered our prayers and gave thanks for all the rescuers, for all being well with our family, and for all creation. A peaceful sleep gently enfolded us. Ah, sweet dreams.

So, there it was, the happiest ending. Wonders never cease.

It took a village to bring about a real lion-hearted victory in the DPNC's plan to renest Wilbur. It's remarkable to consider how many generations of people have experienced similar situations with the nature center since its founding in 1946. One can imagine the legion of rescues and reha- bilitations they have performed for various needy creatures since their establishment. There is a perpetual sound of applause that echoes for them throughout the years, something they so well deserve.

DPNC with surrounding woods in the springtime.

The mission to renest Wilbur also had the vision that he would grow day by day. After about six weeks of age, young owlets start "branching out" onto adjacent tree limbs. At about nine weeks, they are considered fledglings and begin to learn to fly. At ten to twelve weeks, they can fly well. As adults they have wingspans of thirty-five to fifty inches and the highly soft feathers that cover them help to launch a silent flight thereby enabling them to pursue prey and catch them by surprise.

They are one of the longest living owls, and in the wild, their life expectancy is twelve to fifteen years. That's what we all hoped for—that Wilbur and his brother would reach maturity, spread their wings, soar high above while drifting among the clouds, and live a long life.

In captivity, the owls live longer, often into their thirties. One such case was an extraordinary female great horned owl named "ET" (Extra Terrific), born in the southern United States. Someone took her from the wild as a fledgling, but she could

Great Horned Owlet branching out.

Great Horned Fledgling

not be released back into it because she had been "imprinted" by a human being. (She did not have owl parents in her early, formative life to establish owl behavior patterns and recognize and attract her species.)

When ET was a juvenile, she was confiscated by the authorities and sent to a woman known as "The Eagle Lady." She had her

Lori Edwards, Animal Curator, DPNC with ET.

ZBM 1940N

Title:	Wilbur: The Great Horned Owlet's Rescue
Cond:	Very Good
Date:	2024-01-22 16:32:04 (UTC)
mSKU:	ZBM 1940N
vSKU:	ZBV 1977244297 VG
unit_id:	13955818
Source:	CARMEN

federal migratory bird permit and comprehensive avian knowledge, and became the owl's lifetime caretaker. Eventually, she and ET moved to the West Coast.

In April 2019, when no longer able to care for ET, "The Eagle Lady"drove cross-country with the owl to personally transfer her to the DPNC. The animal curator there then became ET's second mom. In 2020, when the coronavirus emerged, they went into lockdown, and during that time, the curator took the owl home to live with her; there she passed away at thirty-eight years old. ET had devoted, expert care throughout her years, was very much loved, and is missed by many.

Over time, the DPNC has had resident owls that have been unable to live in their natural habitat for diverse reasons. Their mascot/logo is a great horned owl named "Mr. Bill." If you ever see one, or any other species of owl, wherever and whenever, maybe you will recall the lives of wee Wilbur and ET. Then take a moment to pause and reflect on these perfect examples

Lori Edwards, Animal Curator with Doris Mager,
"The Eagle Lady," Lifetime Caretaker of ET.

of how we are all linked to wildlife and the natural world. Finding Wilbur and meeting everyone who helped him is an experience I will never forget. The progression of the rescue fell into place like the harmony of notes in a beautiful song, one I will always sing in my mind.

There within are priceless treasures to be cherished and safeguarded. It is our responsibility to persist in being conscientious stewards of them to ensure they continue to thrive for all generations. Nature has always been there for us, and it is vital that we take the time to be there for her. We can start in our personal cosmos, right in our own backyards.

If you can reach out and touch and love and be with wildlife, you will be forever changed. And you will want to make the world a better place. One touch of nature makes the whole world kin. — William Shakespeare

Looking back at that chilly day in March, I found so much beauty and wonder in the world of wildlife. I couldn't have been more surprised by my unexpected meeting, just by chance, with that beguiling owlet, so small and vulnerable. It was like finding a pot of gold at the end of a rainbow.

Then, with every passing hour, the chain of events that developed showed how the many links of kindness and help for Wilbur strengthened the connection between nature and people.

A beautiful quote from a naturalist, cited by the DPNC, says it perfectly:

In every walk with nature, one receives far more than he seeks. —John Muir

Ever since then, I have checked the ground beneath the trees in our yard, especially the pines, to make certain there are no owlets or other baby birds there. And at night, whenever I hear distinctive owl hoots (usually four-to-five "hoot-hoot-hoot-hoot") drifting through the woods and breaking the silence, I will always wonder whether it is Wilbur or a member of his family. That could very well be the case since they are usually nonmigratory, tending to remain in the same general area where they were born, providing there is a good food supply. The males have a lower-pitched voice than the females, so if heard hooting back and forth, it is possible to distinguish them from one another.

To anticipate, not the sunrise and the dawn merely, but, if possible, Nature herself. — Henry David Thoreau

To be in harmony with nature means being observant of nature and wildlife, no matter the time, place, or season. It is of the essence and truly rewarding, leading to more splendid possibilities than we could imagine. Having respect for it and being able to enjoy it is something to celebrate and be thankful for.

Come forth into the light of things, let nature be your teacher. — William Wordsworth

Wilbur's spirit and resilience and his rescuers' perseverance were commendable. We were all privileged to be a part of an unforgettable journey on the road that Wilbur led us down, that simultaneously opened a path to our hearts. Now, that's something to hoot about! Who-o-o could ever forget him?

And, lastly, we will hear from Wilbur:

Wow, I can't believe how my universe turned upside down in just one brief minute. So much happened to me in such a short amount of time! Falling out of my nest was like a nightmare with no hope of being found. But then, unbelievably, I was discovered. I think about how swiftly everyone responded to my dreadful situation. I needed their help, and they were there for me every moment thereafter. I am in awe of them for saving my life. I hope they know how eternally thankful I will be. As I reminisce about all we accomplished together, I surely will miss them, but they will always be in my heart and memory. Might they remember me? I hope so.

Looking to the future, I think about growing up, leaving the nest, and flying free to gaze upon the landscape beneath me. Mom and Dad say it's wonderful to do that. Someday, maybe I'll go to those enchanting woods surrounding the nature center (my second home), choose a towering tree, and start a family of my own. Also, maybe Mr. Bill, the great horned owl that my parents have spoken of, will be there and I will be able to see him.

So now, my friends, it's time for me to say goodbye. I wish health, happiness, and many rainbows of blessings for you. In closing, I would like to make it known that, thanks to each of you, aside from being truly blessed, I believe that I am the luckiest great horned owlet ever!

Hoot-hoot-hooray!

Wilbur

And so, the story of Wilbur came to be.

Soaring Great Horned Owl.

Great Horned Owl
(Bubo virginianus)

Additional Information

They are very adaptable, usually monogamous for life, and live from the Arctic to South America. They are one of the largest owls, second only to the snowy owl.

They favor secluded woodlots, barns, caves or stumps, sides of cliffs, deserts, forests, etc., depending on what part of the country they live in.

Adults sometimes destroy the nest as soon as the young can step up into the tree crotches to make them less conspicuous, thus protecting them from predators.

They have tufts of feathers on their head called "plumicorns," which resemble horns or ears, differentiating them from other owls. They have nothing to do with hearing.

A variable-sized white patch on their throat and brown barred plumage on their underparts give them the popular nickname "tiger owl." This coloring provides good camouflaging when roosting in trees where they like to perch high up near open areas to watch for prey.

Their eyes don't move in their sockets, but instead they can swivel their heads more than 270 degrees in any direction. The eyes are at the front of the head, looking forward, giving them binocular vision. Other birds' eyes are at the sides of the head, giving them a separate range of vision for each eye. Owls have less color vision than other birds.

Great horned owls are alert to the slightest rustle of prey on the ground. From a distance of many feet, they can hear a mouse going through the underbrush and stepping on twigs.

They are considered very useful by humans because they eat many nuisance animals such as rodents.

They don't drink water but get it from their food.

Their digestive system expels pellet-formed material that accumulates at the base of the roosting or nesting tree and can be used by bird-watchers as a guide for finding owls.

They have very powerful and spring-trap locking claws that even an eagle cannot overcome.

For Them, I Am Grateful

The entire magical kingdoms of creatures that inhabit the earth and the oceans play a critical role in keeping us and our planet in balance and thriving. Since the very beginning, humans have been dependent on them in incalculable ways.

Ever since I can remember, nature and wildlife have held a special place in my heart. As many people can attest to, loving and caring for animals, can add so much to our lives, and theirs, a great deal. Our pets were like family members to us, and their unconditional love was touching. Following is a handful of memorable times in which I connected with animals. Without them, necessary strokes of color would have been missing in the landscape of my life. The special love and joy they brought is a gift only they could give.

Growing up, we lived within walking distance of the Bronx Zoo, New York, and it was my mother's favorite place to take my brother, two sisters, and me. After moving to Long Island, New York, we were not able to visit it as often. It was always a part of our lives that never became tiring. The many varieties of beautiful animals there were always a wonder to see and left lasting impressions.

Looking back on the pets we had, one of our dogs, Taffy, was killed by a school bus the day after she had a litter of seven pups, so to feed them, the veterinarian prescribed a formula. The Brownie troop I was in at the time was able to come to our house to feed the pups with baby bottles. They all thrived, and when it was time, we found homes for each of them, except the one we kept. Besides lending a helping hand and loving the pups, the Brownies also earned their pets badge.

As a teenager, I became interested in horses through some close family friends. They had two children, near my age, who had been riding for years because their father was a horse trainer and player on a polo team in Westbury, New York. At first, I was nervous about working with the horses, but I became more relaxed after learning how to feed and groom them, and clean tack (saddles, bridles, reins, etc.). In giving them attention and respect, I became aware of their trust and ease with us as well. We exercised them riding in fields and on trails, often doubling up with another horse on a lead to work more of them at the same time. Years later, that wonderful part of my world came to an end when, sadly, our dear friends moved to another state. Ever since then, I have missed them.

After I was married, I moved to West Mystic, Connecticut, and we got a cat that we named Stanley. A few years later, we moved to Stonington, about five miles away, but within days, Stanley disappeared. About three weeks later, we got a call from our previous neighbor to tell us that he had returned to West Mystic and was on the back porch of the house we left. That seemed impossible! We immediately retrieved him, and we kept him inside our new house longer to help him adjust to the change. That turned out well because it never occurred again.

It has always remained a mystery how Stanley managed to make the trip back to West Mystic. Did he travel over the Mystic River Bridge, which is the shortest, usual route? If not, any other way would have been many miles farther. There are fascinating true stories about pets that have navigated their way home, traveling great distances, and theories on how they accomplished it. These situations illustrate yet another interesting facet of an animal's phenomenal inherent abilities that continue to intrigue humans.

Our first dog, Gretel, was a golden retriever that we had for fourteen years. She was gentle with children, never tired of fetching balls and sticks, and always enjoyed swimming, even in cold weather. One day, a neighbor called to tell us that Gretel ate a pan of lasagna that she had placed outside her door to cool. Of course, we were sorry to hear that and understood her dismay. It reminded us how a dog's natural tendency and curiosity sometimes gets it (and us) in trouble. When Gretel detected the appealing aroma in the air, she tracked it down...and there it was, a delicious meal she couldn't resist. I think she left a happy and very full dog, not realizing the displeasing deed she had done.

At that time, we also had a kitty named Champ who was so sweet and gentle that she wouldn't hurt a flea. Of course, she couldn't resist the temptation of catching mice and leaving them outside the door as a present.

During those years, I quite unexpectedly got back to equines again when some dear friends acquired a horse, Trooper, for their young daughter. They asked if I would like to be a riding partner with her, and naturally, I was thrilled and happily agreed. She loved horses as much as I did. A horse, Bucky (no, he didn't buck), was available for me to ride where Trooper was boarded. The four of us spent many a delightful day riding wooded trails and seeing nature in all seasons while discovering the personalities of our horses. It was glorious sharing those times with her, something I will always remember. Viva la equinos!

After Gretel and Champ passed away, we were without pets for several years and missed having animals, so, we acquired a dog from the pound. She was a mixed breed, about four months old, and we named her Mocha. She took a while to learn not to encounter skunks, and after being sprayed about the third time in one season, I opened the door and said, "Oh no, not again!" Without prompting, she quickly headed upstairs and jumped into the bathtub, apparently remembering her previous routines for getting washed. I chuckled over that for her reasoning. Expecting it wouldn't be the last time she would try to befriend a striped critter, we installed a hot water spigot outside on the house.

About a year later, I acquired a tabby kitten from a yard sale. She looked just like the cat, Cousin Ribby, in Beatrix Potter's

Tale of the Pie and the Patty-Pan, so that's what I named her. She and Mocha became the best of friends; they would play, take naps together, and join me on walks.

When Mocha was about eight years old, she developed a serious health problem. One day she was resting on the front porch, not feeling well, with Ribby beside her when two friendly neighborhood dogs started coming up the driveway. Ribby jumped off the porch and chased them, and they turned around and ran off with their tails between their legs. It was astonishing to think that she knew how ill her pal felt and wanted to protect her.

A few days later, the vet said that there wasn't anything more that could help Mocha and that she was in a lot of pain. Considering this, we decided to do what was best, and we left without her. When we arrived home, Ribby was waiting, and when she saw that Mocha wasn't with us, she seemed to understand what had happened. After that, she lost her appetite and started losing weight, and would walk around the house meowing, seemingly looking for Mocha. I could sense her heartbreak. After bringing her to the vet, he determined that she was depressed and grieving over the loss of her companion. Over the next couple of months, giving her extra attention and care helped her condition gradually improve. However, I believe she never stopped missing Mocha. Seeing her go through this, it seemed evident that she experienced emotions paralleling those of humans.

The following year, Ribby disappeared for about two months, and I was sure I'd never see her again. Then, one day, she appeared at the back door, barely able to walk and extremely thin. It was a sorrowful sight, and obviously, whatever her story was, it must have been very traumatic for her. There was never any clue, nor could I guess what had happened or where she had been all that time, but, remarkably, she recovered once again. It wasn't until she was about eleven years of age that she passed away.

An amusing sidenote to tell is about my son's cat, Mr. Higgins, who was very hungry one morning because his breakfast was late. So, he carried his food bowl upstairs to where my son was, and dropped it on the floor, as if to say, "Feed me now!" How smart was that? Also, having a very friendly nature, he would greet you at the door when you entered the house, exhibiting a more dog-like characteristic. Surely, he was quite the personality kitty.

While living in Connecticut, it has been exciting to see the marvelous wildlife that randomly appears in our yard. We usually scramble to get our camera when there is an opportunity. Although these lists are not totally complete, they include deer, red fox, grey fox, bobcat, coyote, and fisher cat. Of course, there are also the numerous, everyday variety of smaller mammals. Then, there is the wonderful array of waterfowl, white egrets, blue herons, osprey, hawks, wild turkey, peregrine falcons, owls, an eagle that recently appeared, and the wide variety of birds at the feeders. Lately, there have been reports of bear sightings in the local area, but they have not wandered through our property (that we know of).

Camera time, if they do - or, run and hide?

Then...there was the indelible day I incredibly found a tiny bird, and I knew right away it was something special. And now, you know that whole story. I was enthralled with him at first sight, and it didn't take him long to dazzle everyone else who encountered him.

The DPNC staff has so many combined skills that foster their ongoing effectiveness, and obviously, they enter these types of situations with true devotion and caring. It was particularly impressive to observe them working together. Everything that I experienced with them, and others, gave me the inspiration to write about the rescue.

We can follow their lead by individually ensuring the well-being of animals that enter our lives, whether domesticated, wildlife, or both. Each of the animals in my life were special and winsome in their own way, and it was a blessing to have them and care for them. For that, I am grateful.

It can be seen how, throughout the ages, in the most grandeur and in the simplest of ways, Mother Nature can reveal so much splendor to us. Whatever realm it may be, she can give us solace and complement our being in a heartfelt way. If we observe her closely, she will show us more than we ever imagined and never disappoint us. What a gift to behold!

Wilbur's Poem

Cold and blustery, that's how it could be described
    that typical day of northeast March weather,
When I was only a couple of days old and covered
    head to toe with a white coat of soft, downy feathers.

The chilly air persistently swirled about in all directions
    but could not engulf me, no matter how much it tried,
Because Mom wrapped her wings around my brother
    and me to keep us warm, ever there to lovingly abide.

Out of the blue, something caused an invasive ruckus
    and before I knew it, I was falling fast out of my nest,
Frightfully traveling over seventy feet to the ground, yet
    remarkably surviving, so I'm able to tell you the rest.

I was lying there, alone, and afraid, when along came
     footsteps; I was found, and somehow inherently knew
That now I would be safe and sound, and how fortunate
     it was to be rescued, seeming too good to be true.

After a comforting night of getting lots of needed care
     with a heated cozy bed and food, the very next day,
My concerned and dedicated fans worked very hard to
     create a plan that would bring me home all the way.

A bucket lift they did use, and of course it was large and
     unavoidably noisy, causing my parents to disappear.
Happily, even with so much clamor and confusion, they
     were soon visible perching in trees that were near.

After the lift reached my abode, at last, I was reunited
     with my brother and relieved seeing him waiting for me.
We had a lot to tell each other, then very soon, our parents
     returned, making the four of us joyfully chirp with glee.

Being found at the remote spot I fell to was highly unlikely
     and something I know my family and I will never forget.
Ever since then, we've been mighty grateful for all of you
     who helped make the world we share the very best yet.

Something I'd like everyone to please consider is to always
     be observing and listening when you're out and about,
Because quite unexpectedly, there may be that time when,
     There I will be, hooting you a welcoming, thankful shout!

CPSIA information can be obtained
at www.ICGtesting.com
Printed in the USA
BVHW020245290122
627162BV00001B/1